MATH BEHIND THE SCIENCE

Puzzling Out Patterns

REBECCA L. JOHNSON

PICTURE CREDITS
Cover: © Pascal Goetgheluck/Science Photo Library/Photo
Researchers, Inc. Page 1 © Michelle Press/Index Stock Imagery,
Inc.; pages 2–3 © Art Wolfe/Art Wolfe; pages 4 (left), 18 © Tom
Pantages adaptation/courtesy NOAA; page 4 (right) © J. Nettis/
Robertstock.com; pages 4–5, 8 (left), 9 (right) © Ed Degginger/
Color Pic, Inc.; pages 6, 10, 14 Equator Graphics; pages 6–7
© Wolfgang Kaehler/Corbis; pages 8 (right top), 8 (right bottom),
20 (lower left), 21 (lower right), 21 (top right) Royalty-Free/Corbis;
page 9 (left) © Sunset/Brake/Animals Animals; page 9 (right top)
© Carolyn A McKeone/Photo Researchers, Inc.; pages 10–11
© Robert W. Ginn/PhotoEdit; page 12 © Mauro Fermariello/Science
Photo Library/Photo Researchers, Inc.; page 13 © Russell Holloway/
Russell Holloway; pages 14–15 © NOAA; page 17 © W. Haxby,
LDEO/Science Photo Library/Photo Researchers, Inc.; page 19
Precision Graphics; pages 20 (top left), 20–21 (middle), 21
(lower left), 21 (middle), 21 (middle right), 21 (top left), 21 (top middle),
21 (middle left) © Hemera Technologies; pages 20–21 (lower)
© Mark Smith/Photo Researchers, Inc.; page 23 © Brian J. Skerry/
National Geographic Image Collection.

Cover photo: The "eye" pattern in a peacock feather

E-mail addresses and names are fictitious. Any resemblance to an
actual e-mail address or person associated with such address is
entirely coincidental.

Produced through the worldwide resources of the National Geographic
Society, John M. Fahey, Jr., President and Chief Executive Officer;
Gilbert M. Grosvenor, Chairman of the Board; Nina D. Hoffman, Executive
Vice President and President, Books and Education Publishing Group.

PREPARED BY NATIONAL GEOGRAPHIC SCHOOL PUBLISHING
Ericka Markman, Senior Vice President and President, Children's
Books and Education Publishing Group; Steve Mico, Vice President,
Editorial Director; Rosemary Baker, Executive Editor; Barbara Seeber,
Editorial Manager; Jim Hiscott, Design Manager; Kristin Hanneman,
Illustrations Manager; Matt Wascavage, Manager of Publishing Services;
Sean Philpotts, Production Manager.

MANUFACTURING AND QUALITY MANAGEMENT
Christopher A. Liedel, Chief Financial Officer; Phillip L. Schlosser,
Director; Clifton M. Brown, Manager.

PROGRAM DEVELOPER
Kate Boehm Jerome

ART DIRECTION
Daniel Banks, Project Design Company

CONSULTANT/REVIEWER
Mary Cavanagh, Math and Science Project Specialist, San Diego County Office
of Education

BOOK DEVELOPMENT
Navta Associates

Published by the National Geographic Society
1145 17th Street, N.W.
Washington, D.C. 20036-4688

ISBN-13: 978-0-7922-4594-0
ISBN-10: 0-7922-4594-6

Third Printing, June 2012
Printed in Canada

TABLE OF CONTENTS

Puzzles

to Patterns

Do you like number puzzles? Try this: 1, 2, 4, 8, 16, and 32. Can you see a pattern? Doubling each number gives you the next one.

Numbers are a part of science. But the numbers that researchers get from taking measurements and carrying out experiments can be confusing, just like number puzzles. Looking for patterns is one solution. Seeing how numbers are related helps scientists make discoveries about everything from sizes of bird eggs to models of dinosaurs to the shape of the seafloor.

Math is the key to puzzling out number patterns and relationships in science. It's so handy that scientists couldn't function without it. Let's join several scientists who deal with numbers. They are doing research in many parts of the world and sending e-mails to one another. They'll show us the math behind the science.

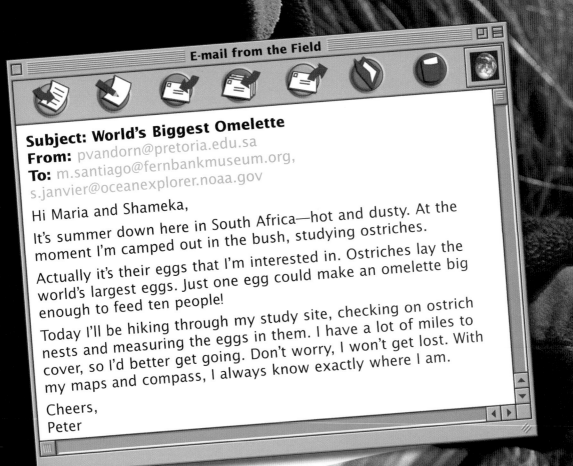

E-mail from the Field

Subject: World's Biggest Omelette
From: pvandorn@pretoria.edu.sa
To: m.santiago@fernbankmuseum.org,
s.janvier@oceanexplorer.noaa.gov

Hi Maria and Shameka,

It's summer down here in South Africa—hot and dusty. At the moment I'm camped out in the bush, studying ostriches.

Actually it's their eggs that I'm interested in. Ostriches lay the world's largest eggs. Just one egg could make an omelette big enough to feed ten people!

Today I'll be hiking through my study site, checking on ostrich nests and measuring the eggs in them. I have a lot of miles to cover, so I'd better get going. Don't worry, I won't get lost. With my maps and compass, I always know exactly where I am.

Cheers,
Peter

ASIA

AFRICA

ATLANTIC
OCEAN

INDIAN
OCEAN

South
Africa

Big Bird

Ostriches are the world's largest living birds. It's not surprising that they lay the world's largest eggs. An ostrich egg is bigger than a grapefruit. It can weigh more than 2 kilograms (4.4 pounds).

The shells of ostrich eggs are nearly one-eighth of an inch thick. These shells need to be strong. Otherwise the eggs would break when the 136-kilogram (300-pound) parent birds sit on them.

Peter has become an ostrich egg expert. He has also studied one of the world's smallest bird eggs. They are laid by the tiny bee hummingbird. How small are bee hummingbird eggs? Believe it or not, 4,700 of them could fit inside an ostrich egg!

Comparing Quantities

A bee hummingbird egg isn't as common as a chicken egg. So when Peter describes how big ostrich eggs are, he compares them to chicken eggs. One ostrich egg could hold about 24 chicken eggs.

Peter expresses this relationship as a **ratio**. A ratio is a comparison of two numbers.

A ratio can be written in several ways. One way is to use ordinary words in a sentence. For example, Peter could say, "One ostrich egg is equal in size to 24 chicken eggs." The word "to" is an important clue that this statement is a ratio.

Saying It With Numbers

But there's an easier way to compare two quantities. By using numbers instead of words, ratios can be expressed much more simply. Peter can write the ratio as 1:24, which is read as "1 to 24." The ratio 1:24 is a mathematical way of stating that 1 ostrich egg is equal to 24 chicken eggs.

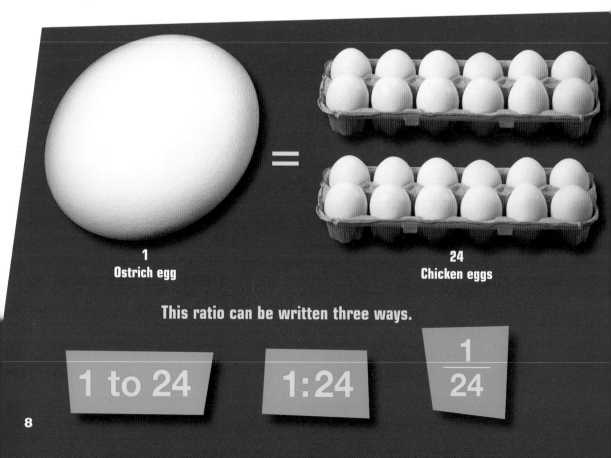

1
Ostrich egg

24
Chicken eggs

This ratio can be written three ways.

1 to 24   **1:24** $\frac{1}{24}$

That same ratio can also be written as a fraction: $\frac{1}{24}$. In other words, a chicken egg is $\frac{1}{24}$ the size of an ostrich egg. You could also turn that around to say that an ostrich egg is 24 times the size of 1 chicken egg. No matter how you say it, though, an ostrich egg is mighty big!

In science, ratios are essential math tools. They show with numbers how one thing relates to another. As you'll see, ratios can help you make sense of what you know—and help you discover what you don't know.

Newborn ostrich chick

E-mail from the Field

Subject: Making Models
From: m.santiago@fernbankmuseum.org
To: pvandorn@pretoria.edu.sa, s.janvier@oceanexplorer.noaa.gov

Hey Peter,

That's one big egg you're studying. As you know, dinosaurs laid eggs, too. We have a skeleton of the dinosaur *Argentinosaurus* on display here in Atlanta at the museum. It may be the largest creature that ever roamed Earth. Imagine how big its eggs must have been!

I'm getting to know *Argentinosaurus* really well. That's because I'm making a model of it for a traveling exhibit. The real one is far too big to move. But before I start building, I have some calculations to make. Math will help me bring *Argentinosaurus* down to a more manageable size.

Maria

An Ancient Giant

The dinosaur *Argentinosaurus* lived about 90 million years ago. Very little is known about this huge dinosaur. Only a few of its fossil bones have been found. They were discovered in Argentina in South America. That's how *Argentinosaurus* got its name.

From those few fossils, scientists were able to make educated guesses about the rest of the dinosaur's bones. Based on their research, they created an *Argentinosaurus* skeleton. It's on display in the Fernbank Museum of Natural History.

Argentinosaurus was nearly 40 meters (130 feet) long, with a long neck and an even longer tail. It may be the biggest dinosaur—and the largest land animal—that ever lived.

A skeleton of *Argentinosaurus* at the Fernbank Museum of Natural History in Atlanta, Georgia

Dino Downsizing

Maria's challenge is to make a **scale model** of *Argentinosaurus*. It will look similar to the actual skeleton of the dinosaur, only smaller. You can buy a model airplane, which is a scale model. But Maria can't buy this dinosaur model in a store. She has to create her own. She can downsize a dinosaur by using ratios!

Maria wants her model to be ten times smaller than the actual *Argentinosaurus* skeleton. So the ratio of the dinosaur skeleton to the model is 10:1. If one of the dinosaur's toe bones is 10 centimeters (4 inches) long, the same bone in the model would be 1 centimeter (.4 inch) long. To help Maria figure out more measurements in her model, she created the ratio table to the right.

What Comes Next?

Do you notice a pattern? Every number in the left-hand column of the table is ten times larger than the corresponding number in the right-hand column. Each number pair reflects the same ratio, which is 10:1.

A ratio table like Maria's can be used to **predict** other numbers in a sequence. It can tell us what we don't know or are trying to find out. If a bone is 60 centimeters (24 inches) long, how long would it be in the model? The next pair of numbers would be 60 and 6. So a bone that is 60 centimeters (24 inches) long will be 6 centimeters (2.4 inches) long in the model.

Scale Model of Argentinosaurus	
Size of Argentinosaurus bones (in cm)	Size of model bones (in cm)
10	1
20	2
30	3
40	4
50	5
Ratio of Dinosaur to Model = 10:1	

A scientist working on a dinosaur model

Scientists piece together *Argentinosaurus* at the Fernbank Museum.

Maria could have spent hours filling in her table with more number pairs. Instead, she came up with a way to find the size of any bone in the model that reflects the 10 to 1 relationship.

If *n* stands for the length of any bone in the real *Argentinosaurus* skeleton, divide that length by ten.

$$n \div 10$$

Let's say a rib of *Argentinosaurus* is 190 centimeters (75 inches) long. Maria simply plugs in 190 for *n* and divides by 10 to get the length of that rib in her model.

$$190 \div 10 = 19$$

The ratio is 190 to 19, which is still a 10 to 1 ratio!

Figuring It Out!

The *Argentinosaurus* skeleton in the Fernbank Museum is about 40 meters (130 feet) long. Can you use *n* ÷ 10 to figure out the length of Maria's scale model?

- The length of the actual dinosaur is 40 meters (130 feet).

- Plug 40 into the equation to get 40 ÷ 10.

- Divide 40 by 10 to get 4.

- The ratio becomes 40 to 4 or 40:4. The length of the model is 4 meters (13 feet).

Subject: Deep-Sea Views
From: s.janvier@oceanexplorer.noaa.gov
To: pvandorn@pretoria.edu.sa, m.santiago@fernbankmuseum.org

Hey Pete and Maria,

Nice to hear from you two. Sorry it took me a while to reply, but I'm on a ship in the Pacific Ocean. Sometimes our e-mail can be pretty slow.

Peter, I know how important maps can be. In fact, I'm out here with a science team making maps of the bottom of the ocean. And we're doing it with sound! Take a look at the picture I've attached. It's part of a seafloor map we made today.

This job makes me feel like an explorer. I'm mapping out a landscape that no one has ever seen before.

Later,
Shameka

NORTH AMERICA

PACIFIC OCEAN

ATLANTIC OCEAN

14

See With Sound

Mapping the seafloor has been a challenge for scientists. After all, how can you see what's in total darkness thousands of meters beneath the ocean's surface?

In the mid-1900s, people used **echosounders** to determine ocean depth. Then **sonar** was introduced. Sonar systems bounce sound off the seafloor and measure the returning echoes. These echoes are turned into "pictures" of what's out of sight underwater. Sonar images reveal not only how far down the seafloor is but also its shape.

Shameka's team is using the latest type of sonar, called side-scanning sonar, to "see" underwater in an entirely new way. With the help of advanced computer graphics, these sonar systems create incredibly detailed maps of the ocean floor.

Sonar image of the seafloor off the coast of California

Timed Travel

It's possible to measure distance using sound because of ratios and number patterns. Scientists know that sound travels pretty fast in seawater, about 1,500 meters (4,920 feet) per second. (That's about 5 times faster than sound travels through air.) If you express that relationship as a ratio, you get 1,500 meters to 1 second, or simply 1,500:1.

Using 1,500:1 as a starting point, you can make a ratio table like the one below. See the pattern? In 1 second, sound travels 1,500 meters in seawater. In 2 seconds, it travels 3,000 meters; in 3 seconds, 4,500 meters; and so on. With each increase of a second, the distance sound travels increases by 1,500 meters.

How far does sound travel through the ocean in 5 seconds? Continuing the pattern in the table, the answer is 7,500 meters (1,500 meters more than 6,000 meters).

Can you make a general equation to express this relationship, like Maria did for her scale model?

Absolutely! In the table the relationship between the distance sound travels underwater compared to time is $n \times 1{,}500{:}n$.

You can use this equation to discover things you don't know. For example, let's say it takes 6 seconds for a sound to travel from point A to point B in the ocean. How far apart are points A and B? Plug 6 into the ratio equation and do the math:

$$n \times 1{,}500{:}n$$
$$6 \times 1{,}500{:}6$$
$$9{,}000{:}6$$

The resulting ratio is 9,000 to 6, or 9,000:6. Here's the answer: points A and B are 9,000 meters (9 kilometers) apart.

Distance Sound Travels Over Time in Seawater	
Meters	**Seconds**
1,500	1
3,000	2
4,500	3
6,000	4
Ratio = 1,500 to 1 or 1,500:1	

This sonar image of the seafloor off the California coast shows that sound travels 9,000 meters (29,500 feet) in 6 seconds.

B 6 seconds

9,000 m (9 km)

A 0 seconds

Great Graphs

There's another way to show the number relationships in a ratio table. You can turn the table into a graph by working with the "distance sound travels through seawater" to "time" ratio (1,500:1). Make a graph that has "time in seconds" for the **x-axis** and "distance in meters" for the **y-axis**.

Next, find 1 on the x-axis and 1,500 on the y-axis. Move across and up to find the point where the two lines intersect. Make a dot. Continue plotting several more points and you will end up with a graph that looks like this.

Pointing the Way to an Answer

Notice how the points on the graph line up neatly along the same diagonal line? That's not just luck! It's the pattern coming through. And you can use this pattern to make predictions. Instead of solving our equation $n \times 1{,}500{:}n$, you can figure out how far sound travels in a certain time—or how much time it takes sound to travel a certain distance—simply by using the graph.

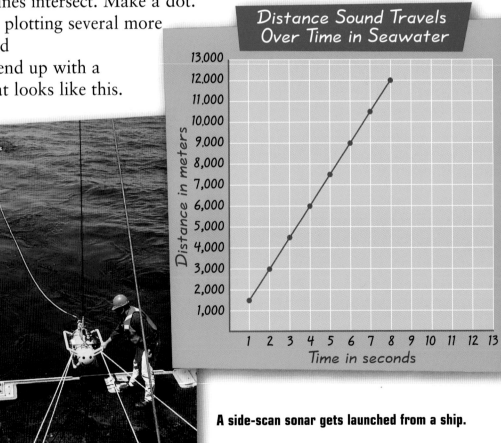

Distance Sound Travels Over Time in Seawater

A side-scan sonar gets launched from a ship.

This picture shows a towed side-scan sonar. A side-scan transmits sound energy and analyzes the return signal. The yellow line on the seafloor highlights the area being scanned.

For example, suppose you want to know the distance a sound travels underwater in 8 seconds. Move your finger up from 8 on the x-axis until you reach the diagonal line. Then go straight across to the y-axis. You'll end up at 12,000. In 8 seconds, a sound travels about 12,000 meters (39,400 feet) underwater.

Maps of the seafloor, like those Shameka makes, are created with the help of sonar, powerful computers, and other high-tech tools. But the math behind the science still reflects the fundamental relationship between how far sound travels underwater in a certain amount of time. The power of the pattern points the way.

Figuring It Out!

Using the graph on page 18, figure out how long it would take a sound to travel 5,000 meters (16,400 feet) through the ocean. Here's how:

- Go up the y-axis to 5,000.

- Move straight across the graph until you hit the diagonal line that connects the other points.

- At that point, move straight down the graph to the x-axis.

- You will come down to about 3.5 on the x-axis. It takes about 3.5 seconds for a sound to travel 5,000 meters in seawater.

Order Is Important!

When you work with ratios, the number that you put first makes a big difference. Order is important because it can change the meaning of a ratio or make the ratio wrong. To make the right comparison in a ratio, you must place the correct number on each side of the colon.

Tip

When you write a ratio, it helps to say aloud what you are comparing to what.

◀ **Sometimes figuring out which number comes first is tricky. Try this tip the next time you compare two things.**

Suppose you are studying saltwater fish. Some fish are blue; some are yellow; some are green.

1 Note the three colors of fish. How many fish are blue? yellow? green?

blue fish 6
yellow fish 4
green fish 1

2 To determine the ratio of blue fish to yellow fish, think about which number should be placed first.

6 blue fish to 4 yellow fish = 6:4

3 Now find the ratio of green fish to blue fish.

1:6

4 Figure out the ratio of yellow fish to green fish.

4:1

Try another one!

What is the ratio of green fish to yellow fish? Of blue fish to green?

Math Notebook

Fun Facts

- The extinct elephant bird from Madagascar laid eggs that were seven times larger than ostrich eggs.

- *Argentinosaurus* was a herbivore, or plant-eater. It probably weighed between 80 and 100 tons.

- Seafloor mapping has revealed that the landscape of the ocean floor is every bit as complex as what we see on dry land. There are tall mountains, deep valleys, and broad, flat plains. The deepest features, which are many kilometers deep, are called trenches.

Books to Read

Caron, Lucille, and Philip M. St. Jacques. *Percents and Ratios*. Enslow Publishers, 2000.

Penny, Malcolm. *How Bats "See" in the Dark*. Benchmark Books, 1997.

Websites to Visit

Visit these websites for more information about some of the science and math topics you've read about in this book.

Investigate the sizes, shapes, and colors of different bird eggs at the Provincial Museum of Alberta's virtual bird exhibition at *www.pma.edmonton.ab.ca/vexhibit/ eggs/vexhome/sizeshap.htm*

Discover the story of *Argentinosaurus*—how it was discovered, how the skeleton was put together, and how the dinosaur found its new home at the Fernbank Museum by visiting *teacher.scholastic.com/activities/ dinosaurs/Argentinosaurus/index.htm*

People are not the only animals that use sound to "see" things underwater. Check out how ocean animals use sound to find food and move through their watery world at *oceanlink.island.net/oinfo/acoustics/ echolocate.html*

Glossary

echosounder – a device that uses sound waves to determine the distance from a ship to the seafloor

predict – to make an educated guess based on evidence or information

ratio – a comparison of two numbers

scale model – a model of something that is similar to the original, only a different size

sonar – a system that uses sound waves to "see" objects underwater. The word "sonar" is short for **so**und **na**vigation and **r**anging.

***x*-axis** – the horizontal line of a graph

***y*-axis** – the vertical line of a graph

Dolphins use their own form of sonar, called echolocation, to find food.

Index